TEAM SPIRIT ®

SMART BOOKS FOR YOUNG FANS

THE CAROLINA PANTHERS

BY
MARK STEWART

NORWOOD HOUSE PRESS

CHICAGO, ILLINOIS

Norwood House Press
P.O. Box 316598
Chicago, Illinois 60631

For information regarding Norwood House Press, please visit our website at:
www.norwoodhousepress.com or call 866-565-2900.

All photos courtesy of Getty Images except the following:
Icon SMI (4, 31, 32), Black Book Partners (6, 8, 9, 10, 11, 14, 15, 17, 18, 20,
21, 22, 26, 28, 34 right, 35 top left and bottom, 36, 37, 39, 40, 42 bottom, 43 both, 45),
The Upper Deck Company (23), Carolina Panthers (33),
Topps, Inc. (34 left, 35 top right, 42 top), Matt Richman (48).
Cover Photo: Icon SMI

The memorabilia and artifacts pictured in this book are presented for educational and informational purposes,
and come from the collection of the author.

Editor: Mike Kennedy
Designer: Ron Jaffe
Project Management: Black Book Partners, LLC.
Special thanks to Topps, Inc.

Library of Congress Cataloging-in-Publication Data

Stewart, Mark, 1960-
   The Carolina Panthers / by Mark Stewart.
     p. cm. -- (Team spirit)
   Includes bibliographical references and index.
   Summary: "A revised Team Spirit Football edition featuring the Carolina
Panthers that chronicles the history and accomplishments of the team.
Includes access to the Team Spirit website which provides additional
information and photos"-- Provided by publisher.
   ISBN 978-1-59953-516-6 (library edition : alk. paper) -- ISBN
978-1-60357-458-7 (ebook) 1. Carolina Panthers (Football
team)--History--Juvenile literature. I. Title.
   GV956.C27S74 2012
   796.332'640975676--dc23
                                            2012018798

Manufactured in the United States of America in North Mankato, Minnesota.
205N—082012

COVER PHOTO: Two Panthers jump for joy after a good play.

Table of Contents

QUALITY 1-29-13

ABOUT OUR GLOSSARY

In this book, there may be several words that you are reading for the first time. Some are sports words, some are new vocabulary words, and some are familiar words that are used in an unusual way. All of these words are defined on page 46. Throughout the book, sports words appear in **bold type**. Regular vocabulary words appear in ***bold italic type***.

Meet the Panthers

When a panther stalks its prey, it patiently watches and waits for the perfect moment to strike. Then it pounces with awesome power and speed. This is how the Carolina Panthers play football. They are intelligent, quick, and dangerous. The Panthers can score from anywhere on the field, and their defense is always on the attack.

Playing this type of football takes great confidence and talent. That's not a problem for the Panthers. The team looks for players with special skills who understand that they can be most successful when working toward the same goal. This has always been the winning *formula* for Carolina.

This book tells the story of the Panthers. They are talented, they are smart, and they are patient. In other words, the Panthers live up to their name every time they take the field. The Panthers always come to play hard—and to win.

Jonathan Stewart watches as Steve Smith and Cam Newton celebrate a great play during the 2011 season.

Glory Days

here was a time in the **National Football League (NFL)** when the Carolinas—North and South—were not considered a good place to put a team. A businessman named Jerry Richardson believed the exact opposite. He knew that fans in the area were eager to get their own NFL team. He made it his mission to turn that wish into reality.

Richardson convinced the league that Charlotte, North Carolina, was the perfect city for a new team. The fans agreed. When they heard about Richardson's plan, more than 40,000 of them promised to buy **season tickets**. Construction began on a beautiful new stadium, and the Panthers took the field for the first time in 1995.

The Panthers built their team by selecting unwanted players from other teams and finding young stars in the **draft**. The first player signed by the Panthers was a speedy defensive back named Rod Smith. Their quarterback was **rookie** Kerry Collins. Carolina left no stone unturned. One of the players cut in the team's first training camp was Bill Goldberg. He went on to become a champion in *professional* wrestling.

Carolina's first coach was Dom Capers. He immediately turned the Panthers into a great defensive team. Linebacker Sam Mills was the team's leader on the field. He returned an interception for a touchdown against the New York Jets to give the Panthers their first victory. Carolina won seven games in all that first year, including four in a row. No *expansion team* had ever done that before.

In 1996, the Panthers added four key players: linebacker Kevin Greene, receiver Muhsin Muhammad, running back Tim Biakabutuka, and tight end Wesley Walls. They joined a talented roster that included Eric Davis, Lamar Lathon, Michael Bates, and John Kasay. Amazingly, the Panthers went 12–4 during the regular

LEFT: Kerry Collins warms up before a game.
ABOVE: Sam Mills gets a hug from a teammate.

season and finished first in their **division** of the **National Football Conference (NFC)**. Carolina made the **playoffs** in just its second season.

In their first **postseason** game ever, the Panthers beat the Dallas Cowboys. Suddenly they were playing for the NFC championship and a chance to go to the **Super Bowl**. In the title game, the Panthers took a lead over the Green Bay Packers in the second quarter, but they lost, 30–13.

NFL fans were amazed by Carolina's quick success. Opponents knew the league had a new championship *contender*. Over the next few years, the Panthers put some excellent players on the field, including quarterback Jake Delhomme and running backs Stephen Davis and DeShaun Foster. Steve Smith was Carolina's most dangerous weapon. The speedy receiver could score from anywhere on the field. On defense, the team relied on Dan Morgan, Kris Jenkins, Mike Rucker, Julius Peppers, Mike Minter, and Brentson Buckner.

In 2003, the Panthers went 11–5 and finished first in the **NFC South**. They faced the Cowboys again in the first round of the

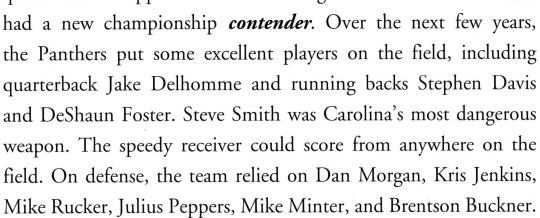

LEFT: Steve Smith snags a pass with one hand.
ABOVE: Jake Delhomme spots an open teammate.

playoffs and beat them for a second time. Next, Carolina won tough games on the road against the St. Louis Rams and then against the Philadelphia Eagles in the **NFC Championship Game**. Seven years after missing a trip to the Super Bowl, the Panthers made it on their second try.

In the seasons that followed, Carolina had good years and bad years. The Panthers won the NFC South twice more, in 2005 and 2008. In 2005, they made it back to the NFC Championship Game, but this time they fell to the Seattle Seahawks. A new generation of stars went into battle for the team, including linebacker Jon Beason, linemen Ryan Kalil and Jordan Gross, and running backs Jonathan Stewart and DeAngelo Williams.

Carolina fell on hard times in 2010. After winning just two games that season, the Panthers decided that they needed one extraordinary player to reverse their fortunes. They decided to draft Cam Newton, a quarterback who had led Auburn University to the top of college football. Newton had remarkable running and passing skills. The NFL had never seen a quarterback quite like him.

In his first year with the Panthers, Newton was nothing short of fantastic. He smashed team records and several league marks for rookie quarterbacks. Between running and passing, Newton accounted for 35 touchdowns and almost 5,000 yards. With their young stars learning and growing each season, the Panthers—and their fans—expect to be Super Bowl contenders year after year.

LEFT: Jonathan Stewart
ABOVE: DeAngelo Williams

Home Turf

The Panthers' stadium was not finished in time for the team's first season. Instead, they played in Memorial Stadium in Greenville, South Carolina. They shared it with the Clemson University football team.

In 1996, the Panthers moved into their current home in Charlotte. Among its most notable features are huge archways and domed towers. When the stadium opened, it was considered way ahead of its time in terms of its technology and *architecture*. In fact, many of the teams that have built new stadiums in recent years based their design on Carolina's.

BY THE NUMBERS

- The Panthers' stadium has 73,778 seats.
- From the field to the top of the scoreboards, the stadium measures 13 stories, or 180 feet.
- Three practice fields are located next to the stadium. Two are grass, and one is artificial turf.

The Charlotte skyline rises above the Panthers' stadium.

Dressed for Success

The Panthers are one of the most stylish teams in the NFL. Their colors are "Panther blue," silver, and black. They normally wear one of two jerseys—one is mostly black, and the other is mostly white. The team chooses white at home when the weather is warm. That forces visiting teams to wear dark uniforms that can make them hotter in the sun. The Panthers also occasionally wear a jersey that is Panther blue.

The team's *logo* pays tribute to the Carolinas. It shows a full-length panther that is the same shape as the states of North Carolina and South Carolina put together. On their helmet, the Panthers use only the head of the panther. It was updated in 2012 to look a bit more modern.

LEFT: Chris Gamble wears the team's Panther blue home uniform.
RIGHT: Wesley Walls waits for a pass in the uniform from the Panthers' 1996 season.

15

We Won!

In the NFL, building a winning team is usually a long, slow process. However, in just their second season, the Panthers won their division and reached the 1996 NFC Championship Game. It was a magical year for coach Dom Capers and his team. Quarterback Kerry Collins provided steady leadership, and the defense punished opponents. Sam Mills made tackles all over the field. Lamar Lathon and Kevin Greene terrorized opposing quarterbacks. Eric Davis and Chad Cota each had five **interceptions**. The future looked bright.

Over the next five years, however, the team failed to have another winning season. In 2002, the Panthers hired John Fox to coach the team. He focused on rebuilding the defense. Carolina already had several stars in Mike Rucker, Kris Jenkins, Dan Morgan, Brentson Buckner, and Mike Minter. In the draft that

LEFT: Dom Capers and Lamar Lathon celebrate a Panthers' playoff victory in 1996.
RIGHT: Julius Peppers holds the jersey showing that Carolina took him with its first pick in the 2002 draft.

year, the Panthers added a player who gave the team a new weapon on defense. His name was Julius Peppers, and he was almost impossible to block.

On offense, the Panthers made two important additions. Running back Stephen Davis was brought in to energize the rushing attack. Jake Delhomme became the starting quarterback. In no time, Delhomme developed good chemistry with Carolina's two best receivers, Muhsin Muhammad and Steve Smith.

The Panthers started the 2003 season a perfect 5–0. Four of these victories came in close, exciting games. Two were won in **overtime**. Soon, Fox had his players believing that they could beat any team in the NFC. That included the St. Louis Rams and Philadelphia Eagles. For most of the year, the experts were convinced that these two teams would meet for the conference title.

The Panthers finished the regular season at 11–5 and won the NFC South. They faced the Dallas Cowboys in the first round of the playoffs and rolled to a 29–10 victory. Davis had a big day with

104 yards and a touchdown. Next up were the Rams. The Carolina defense was sensational. St. Louis had a high-scoring offense, but the Panthers turned the contest into a battle of **field goals**.

The game was tied 23–23 at the end of 60 minutes. Neither team scored in the first overtime period. On the first play of the second overtime, Delhomme dropped back to pass and saw Smith running free in the middle of the field. He made a perfect throw, and the speedy receiver went 69 yards for the winning score. With the victory, Carolina returned to the NFC Championship Game.

This time, they met the Eagles in Philadelphia. The Panthers struck first with a 79-yard touchdown drive in the second quarter. Muhammad got Carolina on the scoreboard with a 24-yard pass from Delhomme. A few minutes later, Rucker made a big hit on Donovan McNabb. The Philadelphia

quarterback struggled the rest of the way and threw four interceptions. Ricky Manning Jr. had three of them.

In the second half, a short touchdown run by DeShaun Foster gave Carolina a 14–3 lead. That was the final score. The Panthers were NFC champions in just their ninth season—and just two seasons after finishing 1–15. The team's dream of winning the Super Bowl fell just short against the New England Patriots. In a thrilling game, the Panthers tied the score with just over a minute left. Unfortunately, the Patriots kicked a field goal as time ran out for a 32–29 victory.

LEFT: Stephen Davis   **ABOVE**: Muhsin Muhammad celebrates a touchdown in the Super Bowl against the New England Patriots.

Go-To Guys

To be a true star in the NFL, you need more than fast feet and a big body. You have to be a "go-to guy"—someone the coach wants on the field at the end of a big game. Panthers fans have had a lot to cheer about over the years, including these great stars ...

THE PIONEERS

JOHN KASAY   Kicker

• BORN: 10/27/1969   • PLAYED FOR TEAM: 1995 TO 2010

John Kasay was Carolina's kicker for the team's first 16 seasons. In 1996, he set an NFL record with 37 field goals. Kasay left the Panthers as their all-time leading scorer.

SAM MILLS   Linebacker

• BORN: 6/3/1959   • DIED: 4/18/2005
• PLAYED FOR TEAM: 1995 TO 1997

Sam Mills was one of the most *inspirational* players in team history. In his three seasons with Carolina, he was the only Panther to start every game. Mills played in the **Pro Bowl** and was voted **All-Pro** in 1996.

KEVIN GREENE   Linebacker

- BORN: 7/31/1962   • PLAYED FOR TEAM: 1996 & 1998 TO 1999

Nothing gave Kevin Greene more joy than tackling the quarterback. His enthusiasm rubbed off on his teammates. In three seasons with the Panthers, Greene had 41.5 **sacks**.

MICHAEL BATES   Kick Returner

- BORN: 12/19/1969   • PLAYED FOR TEAM: 1996 TO 2000

It takes a special player to be a star on **special teams** in the NFL. Michael Bates won a bronze medal in the 200-meter dash at the 1992 *Olympics* and was honored as the NFL's best kick returner of the 1990s.

WESLEY WALLS   Tight End

- BORN: 3/26/1966   • PLAYED FOR TEAM: 1996 TO 2002

Wesley Walls gave the Panthers a great receiving weapon at tight end. He caught 324 passes and scored 44 touchdowns for Carolina. He went to the Pro Bowl five times.

MUHSIN MUHAMMAD   Receiver

- BORN: 5/5/1973   • PLAYED FOR TEAM: 1996 TO 2004

Muhsin Muhammad was tall, smart, and athletic. He had a knack for making great catches. In 2004, Muhammad led all NFL receivers with 1,405 yards and 16 touchdowns.

LEFT: John Kasay
RIGHT: Muhsin Muhammad

MIKE RUCKER   Defensive End

- BORN: 2/28/1975   • PLAYED FOR TEAM: 1999 TO 2007

Mike Rucker was amazingly *agile* for a man his size. He could stop the

run and rush the passer. Twice he made a tackle in the end zone for a **safety**.

DAN MORGAN   Linebacker

- BORN: 12/19/1978
- PLAYED FOR TEAM: 2001 TO 2007

Dan Morgan was big, strong, and fast. Unfortunately, injuries ended his career early. His best season came in 2004 when he intercepted two passes, recovered two **fumbles**, and made the Pro Bowl.

STEVE SMITH   Receiver

- BORN: 5/12/1979   • FIRST YEAR WITH TEAM: 2001

Steve Smith always played like he had something to prove. No receiver in the NFL was more explosive. In 2011, at the age of 32, he averaged 17.6 yards a catch and scored seven touchdowns.

JULIUS PEPPERS   Defensive End

- BORN: 1/18/1986   • PLAYED FOR TEAM: 2002 TO 2007

Julius Peppers was a running back in high school. With the Panthers, he was a defensive superstar. He had 81 sacks for Carolina and was an All-Pro four times.

JON BEASON   Linebacker

• BORN: 1/14/1985   • FIRST YEAR WITH TEAM: 2007

Jon Beason was a speedy linebacker with a knack for causing **turnovers**. He entered the NFL with a bang by finishing second among all rookies in tackles in 2007. Beason was an All-Pro in 2008. In 2011, the Panthers made him the highest-paid linebacker in league history.

RYAN KALIL   Offensive Lineman

• BORN: 3/29/1985   • FIRST YEAR WITH TEAM: 2007

The Panthers drafted Ryan Kalil to be the leader of their offensive line. He developed into one of the strongest and fastest centers in the NFL. Kalil was picked for the Pro Bowl each year from 2009 to 2011.

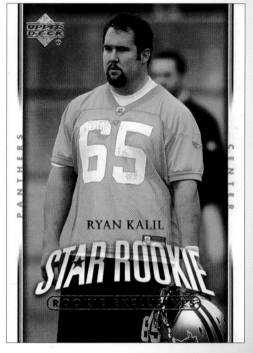

CAM NEWTON   Quarterback

• BORN: 5/9/1989   • FIRST YEAR WITH TEAM: 2011

Rookie quarterbacks normally struggle in their first NFL season. That wasn't the case with Cam Newton. He combined an extraordinary set of skills to become one of the league's most entertaining players. In 2011, Newton threw for 4,051 yards to set a record for first-year players. He also ran for 14 touchdowns, the most ever by a quarterback.

LEFT: Dan Morgan
ABOVE: Ryan Kalil

Calling the Shots

The people who run a football team are often just as important as the players. From the very beginning, the Panthers have spent time making sure they have the right leaders on the sideline and off the field. Team owner Jerry Richardson learned this lesson in the 1950s and 1960s. After playing for the Baltimore Colts, Richardson left football and opened a Hardee's restaurant in 1961. He helped build the fast-food chain into one of the world's largest.

Early in Carolina's history, Richardson surrounded himself with great football minds, including Bill Polian and Mike McCormack. Polian had helped turn the Buffalo Bills into a Super Bowl team. McCormack was a member of the Cleveland Browns during the 1950s, when they were the best team in football. They helped Richardson build a talented roster and find smart coaches.

Dom Capers was the team's first coach. He was a defensive genius who taught his players to work hard and be aggressive. Capers led the Panthers to the NFC Championship Game in just their second season.

John Fox gets a "victory shower" from his players.

After Carolina went 1–15 in 2002, the team turned to John Fox. Like Capers, he specialized in defense. Fox transformed the Panthers, making them one of the most dangerous teams in the NFL. In Fox's second season as coach, Carolina won the NFC championship and played in the Super Bowl for the first time.

In 2011, the Panthers turned to another coach who had experience building great defenses. Ron Rivera had been a linebacker for the Chicago Bears and later coached their defense. In 2006, the Bears made it all the way to the Super Bowl. The Panthers hired Rivera to bring that same winning attitude to Carolina. Rivera was just the third Latino head coach in NFL history and the first since the 1990s.

One Great Day

As the Panthers prepared to play the St. Louis Rams in the 2003 playoffs, football experts gave Carolina little chance to win. The Rams were the second-highest scoring team in the NFL. At home, they were nearly unstoppable.

Even so, the Panthers weren't afraid. Carolina slowed down the Rams with a great defensive effort led by Kris Jenkins and Julius Peppers. Meanwhile, the offense moved the ball well on the ground and through the air. The Panthers built a 23–12 lead with six minutes left in the game, only to see the Rams come charging back. St. Louis tied the score and sent the game into overtime.

The Panthers had the first chance to win, but a penalty ended the opportunity. Minutes

26

later, the Rams missed a kick from 53 yards away. With time running out in the extra period, Ricky Manning Jr. intercepted a pass as the Rams were driving for the winning score. Two plays later, the referees whistled the end of the first overtime. It was already the longest playoff game in NFC history!

Moments later, Jake Delhomme spotted Steve Smith slanting toward the middle of the field. Delhomme fired a pass that Smith caught in stride near the 50-yard line. He squeezed between the two Rams trying to tackle him and sprinted for the end zone. The St. Louis crowd watched in stunned silence as the Panthers celebrated their sudden and spectacular 29–23 victory.

LEFT: Kris Jenkins
ABOVE: Jake Delhomme

Legend Has It

Which Panther was named after two basketball superstars?

LEGEND HAS IT that Julius Peppers was. He was born Julius Frazier Peppers—named after basketball stars Julius Erving and Walt Frazier. Peppers was a great basketball player himself. He played at the University of North Carolina, partly because his hero, Michael Jordan, had gone there. In fact, only in college did Pepper give up his dream of playing pro basketball and focus on the NFL.

ABOVE: Julius Frazier Peppers

Who was the "biggest hitter" on the Panthers?

LEGEND HAS IT that tight end Gary Barnidge was. In 2011, the Panthers were invited to take batting practice with the local baseball team, the Charlotte Knights. Barnidge socked two balls out of the park and was awarded a championship belt by his teammates. The Panthers were invited back in 2012, and Barnidge cracked another homer. Later, he revealed that he'd left the championship belt at home—just in case he was outhit by a teammate. "I didn't bring it because I wasn't giving it up!" he admitted.

Which Panther became an NFL star two seasons after breaking his neck?

LEGEND HAS IT that Steve Smith did. After being tackled on a punt return during a 1999 college game, Smith felt a strange tingle in his neck and shoulders. He played the rest of the game without knowing that he had a serious injury. That night, doctors placed Smith in a special head brace to keep his neck from moving. He wore it for 10 weeks. They told him there was a good chance that he would never play football again. By 2001, Smith was fully recovered. He starred for the Panthers that season and was selected to play in the Pro Bowl.

When Cam Newton was named Carolina's starting quarterback in September of 2011, the fans weren't sure what to expect. The 22-year-old rookie had been a big star in college. However, there were questions about Newton as he began his first NFL season. Could he succeed as a pro?

In his first game, Newton completed 24 of 37 passes and set an NFL record for rookies with 422 passing yards. The only thing that kept Newton's *debut* from being a complete success was the fact that Carolina lost to the Arizona Cardinals. One week later, the Panthers faced the Green Bay Packers, the previous year's Super Bowl champions. They were ready for Newton—or so they thought. When the final seconds ticked off the clock, Carolina fans could hardly believe what they had just seen. Newton torched the Green Bay defense for 432 yards to break his week-old record. Unfortunately, the Panthers lost again.

Newton finally got his first win a week later, when Carolina beat the Jacksonville Jaguars 16–10. He led the Panthers to five more victories in 2011. As the season progressed, opponents tried to find new ways

Cam Newton celebrates a touchdown with his teammates
during the 2011 season.

to stop Newton and the Carolina passing game. He crossed them up
by running the ball more often. He finished the year with 706 rushing
yards and 14 touchdowns. He also broke Peyton Manning's record for
passing yards by a rookie, with 4,051.

Newton's greatest game may have been his 38–19 victory over the
Tampa Bay Buccaneers in December. During that contest, he ran
for three touchdowns and also threw a touchdown pass to Legedu
Naanee. Newton was almost part of a fifth touchdown when he
caught a pass from Naanee on a trick play. He was tackled just short
of the end zone.

Team Spirit

Before the Panthers came to town, many people in the Carolinas rooted for the Washington Redskins. When the two teams play, it creates a lot of excitement. Now the Panthers are the region's favorite NFL team. Carolina draws fans from all over the South, including Georgia, Tennessee, Kentucky, West Virginia, Virginia, and, of course, North Carolina and South Carolina.

Fans of the Panthers are some of the most devoted in the NFL. They are known for their fancy tailgate parties, and many dress in Panther blue and silver for games. It took 75 years for the NFL to place a team in the Carolinas, and the fans always try to show it was a great decision by filling the stadium for every home game.

Carolina fans have plenty to cheer about when the Panthers play. The team's *mascot*, Sir Purr, roams the stadium and has lots of fun with the crowd. The TopCats dance team is one of the league's best.

LEFT: Carolina fans love to wear their team colors.
ABOVE: This 1997 guide book shows Sam Mills in action.

Timeline

In this timeline, each Super Bowl is listed under the year it was played. Remember that the Super Bowl is held early in the year and is actually part of the previous season. For example, Super Bowl XLVI was played on February 5, 2012, but it was the championship of the 2011 NFL season.

1996
The Panthers play for the NFC title.

2002
Jullius Peppers is voted Defensive Rookie of the Year.

1995
The Panthers play their first season.

1999
Steve Beuerlein leads the NFL with 4,436 passing yards.

2001
Punter Todd Sauerbrun is named All-Pro.

Steve Beuerlein

Todd Sauerbrun

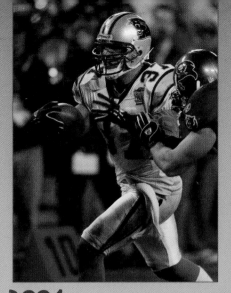

Nick Goings was a member of the Super Bowl team.

Jon Beason

2004

The Panthers play in Super Bowl XXXVII.

2010

Jon Beason makes the Pro Bowl for the third time.

2005

Steve Smith leads the NFL with 103 receptions.

2008

DeAngelo Williams leads the NFL with 18 touchdowns.

2011

Cam Newton is named Offensive Rookie of the Year.

DeAngelo Williams takes a handoff from Jake Delhomme.

Fun Facts

SMOOTH SWITCH

In 2010, injuries to the Carolina defense forced Jon Beason to switch positions. He moved from inside linebacker to outside linebacker. Beason adjusted so quickly that he was named to the Pro Bowl at his new position.

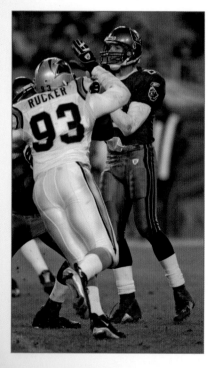

CREATING A RUCKUS

In 2005, Mike Rucker started a child learning center called Ruckus House. His partners were fellow Panthers Mike Minter, Muhsin Muhammad, and Stephen Davis. Ruckus House now has two schools in North Carolina.

PLEASE, NO TURNOVERS!

In 2011, the Panthers had a 6–10 record. In games when Cam Newton did not fumble or throw an interception, they were a perfect 6–0. In games when he did, Carolina's record was 0–10!

LET HIM HEAR IT

Hardworking fullback Brad Hoover played for the Panthers from 2000 to 2009. He became one of Carolina's most beloved players for the way he flattened opponents with bone-rattling blocks. Whenever he made a good play, fans would chant, "HOOOOOOOOVER!"

GOING LONG

In Super Bowl XXXVIII, Jake Delhomme threw an 85-yard touchdown pass to Muhsin Muhammad. The scoring strike set a record for the longest passing play in Super Bowl history.

CUTTING IT CLOSE

In 2003, the Panthers were nicknamed the "Cardiac Cats" because of their many heart-pounding victories. They tied two NFL records by winning seven games by three points or fewer and three games in overtime.

LEFT: Mike Rucker
ABOVE: Brad Hoover

Talking Football

"I never had any doubts that we would play in the Super Bowl."
► **Jerry Richardson,** *on building the Panthers into a championship team*

"It's a great feeling to be a Carolina Panther."
► **Cam Newton,** *on joining the Panthers*

"Some guys are athletes, some guys are big, some guys are mean. He's a football player."
► **Mike Minter,** *on Jon Beason*

"I'm the only one who truly knows the ability I have."
► **Julius Peppers,** *on why he always worked hard to improve*

"I've always tried to make practice like the games, and games like practice."

▶ **John Kasay**, *on preparing to make kicks under pressure*

"I'm not the tallest guy. I've got to go and attack the ball."

▶ **Steve Smith**, *on his great leaping catches*

"It's a great group of guys. I wanted to do anything I could to stay here."

▶ **Dan Morgan**, *on why he spent his whole career with Carolina*

"If you weren't doing a good job, he told you and told you how you had to do it the next time—or else."

▶ **Brentson Buckner**, *on coach John Fox*

LEFT: Jerry Richardson
ABOVE: John Kasay

Great Debates

People who root for the Panthers love to compare their favorite moments, teams, and players. Some debates have been going on for years! How would you settle these classic football arguments?

Jake Delhomme was Carolina's greatest quarterback ...

... because he guided the team to its first Super Bowl—and nearly won the game! Delhomme (LEFT) was a backup quarterback for the New Orleans Saints for many years before becoming Carolina's starter. His leadership turned the Panthers into a championship contender. He also played in the Pro Bowl after the 2005 season.

Hold on! No one beats Cam Newton ....

... because he broke one rookie record after another in 2011. His ability to throw long, accurate passes and run for touchdowns when his receivers were covered sometimes made it seem as if the Panthers had an extra player on the field. More important, Newton made the team believe it could beat anyone. He loved the pressure of trailing in the fourth quarter and leading Carolina to victory.

The greatest play in team history was DeShaun Foster's touchdown run in the 2003 playoffs ....

... because it got the Panthers into the Super Bowl. Carolina held a slim 7–3 lead over the Philadelphia Eagles in the third quarter of the 2003 NFC Championship Game. The Panthers had the ball on the 1-yard line. Jake Delhomme handed off to Foster, who ran toward the right corner of the end zone. The Eagles were waiting for him with five tacklers. Foster blasted through them and tumbled into the end zone. The Panthers won 14–3 and were NFC champs!

Nothing could top Steve Smith's 69-yard touchdown a week earlier in the 2003 playoffs ....

... because it beat the powerhouse St. Louis Rams in double-overtime. Smith (RIGHT) saved the day with his score. The Panthers had blown an 11-point lead in the fourth quarter. A lot of Carolina fans thought their season was over. However, the defense held the Rams in the first overtime period, and Smith gave the Panthers the victory that kept their Super Bowl hopes alive. They never would have faced the Eagles if not for this play!

For the Record

The great Panthers teams and players have left their marks on the record books. These are the "best of the best" …

Cam Newton

PANTHERS AWARD WINNERS

WINNER	AWARD	YEAR
Dom Capers	Coach of the Year	1996
Julius Peppers	Defensive Rookie of the Year	2002
Cam Newton	Offensive Rookie of the Year	2011

Julius Peppers

PANTHERS ACHIEVEMENTS

ACHIEVEMENT	YEAR
NFC West Champions	1996
NFC South Champions	2003
NFC Champions	2003
NFC South Champions	2005
NFC South Champions	2008

RIGHT: Stephen Davis ran for 1,444 yards in 2003.

BELOW: Steve Smith led the 2008 team with 78 catches.

Pinpoints

The history of a football team is made up of many smaller stories. These stories take place all over the map—not just in the city a team calls "home." Match the pushpins on these maps to the **Team Facts**, and you will begin to see the story of the Panthers unfold!

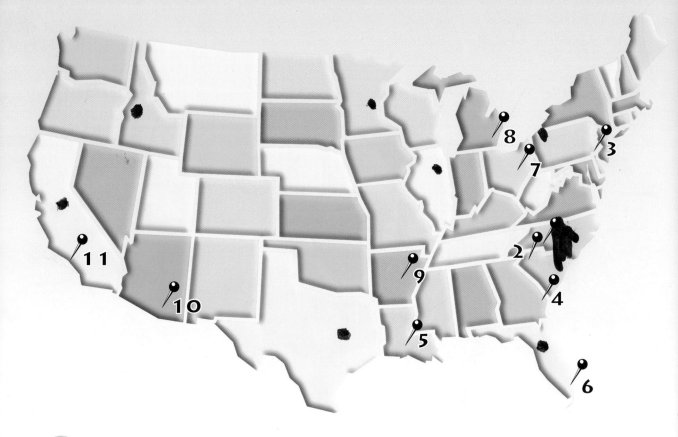

TEAM FACTS

1 Charlotte, North Carolina—*The Panthers have played here since 1996.*

2 Greenville, South Carolina—*The Panthers played here in their first season.*

3 Philadelphia, Pennsylvania—*The Panthers won the 2003 NFC championship here.*

4 Savannah, Georgia—*Cam Newton was born here.*

5 Breaux Bridge, Louisiana—*Jake Delhomme was born here.*

6 Coral Springs, Florida—*Dan Morgan was born here.*

7 Cambridge, Ohio—*Dom Capers was born here.*

8 Ypsilanti, Michigan—*Kris Jenkins was born here.*

9 Little Rock, Arkansas—*DeAngelo Williams was born here.*

10 Tucson, Arizona—*Michael Bates was born here.*

11 Los Angeles, California—*Steve Smith was born here.*

12 Kinshasa, Democratic Republic of the Congo—*Tim Biakabutuka was born here.*

Tim Biakabutuka

Glossary

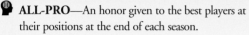

AGILE—Quick and graceful.

ALL-PRO—An honor given to the best players at their positions at the end of each season.

ARCHITECTURE—The structure or design of a building.

CONTENDER—A person or team that competes for a championship.

DEBUT—First appearance.

DIVISION—A group of teams that play in the same part of the country.

DRAFT—The annual meeting during which NFL teams choose from a group of the best college players.

EXPANSION TEAM—A team that is new to a league.

FIELD GOALS—Goals from the field, kicked over the crossbar and between the goal posts. A field goal is worth three points.

FORMULA—A set way of doing something.

FUMBLES—Balls that are dropped by the players carrying them.

INSPIRATIONAL—Giving positive and confident feelings to others.

INTERCEPTIONS—Passes that are caught by the defensive team.

LOGO—A symbol or design that represents a company or team.

MASCOT—An animal or person believed to bring a group good luck.

NATIONAL FOOTBALL CONFERENCE (NFC)—One of two groups of teams that make up the NFL.

NATIONAL FOOTBALL LEAGUE (NFL)—The league that started in 1920 and is still operating today.

NFC CHAMPIONSHIP GAME—The game played to determine which NFC team will go to the Super Bowl.

NFC SOUTH—A division for teams that play in the southern part of the country.

OLYMPICS—An international sports competition held every four years.

OVERTIME—The extra period played when a game is tied after 60 minutes.

PLAYOFFS—The games played after the regular season to determine which teams play in the Super Bowl.

POSTSEASON—Another term for playoffs.

PRO BOWL—The NFL's all-star game, played after the regular season.

PROFESSIONAL—Paid to play.

ROOKIE—A player in his first year.

SACKS—Tackles of the quarterback behind the line of scrimmage.

SAFETY—A tackle of a ball carrier in his own end zone. A safety is worth two points.

SEASON TICKETS—Packages of tickets for each home game.

SPECIAL TEAMS—The groups of players who take the field for punts, kickoffs, field goals, and extra points.

SUPER BOWL—The championship of the NFL, played between the winners of the National Football Conference and American Football Conference.

TURNOVERS—Fumbles or interceptions that give possession of the ball to the opposing team.

OVERTIME

TEAM SPIRIT introduces a great way to stay up to date with your team! Visit our **OVERTIME** link and get connected to the latest and greatest updates. **OVERTIME** serves as a young reader's ticket to an exclusive web page—with more stories, fun facts, team records, and photos of the Panthers. Content is updated during and after each season. The **OVERTIME** feature also enables readers to send comments and letters to the author! Log onto:

www.norwoodhousepress.com/library.aspx

and click on the tab: **TEAM SPIRIT** to access **OVERTIME**.

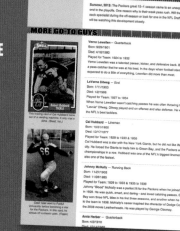

Read all the books in the series to learn more about professional sports. For a complete listing of the baseball, basketball, football, and hockey teams in the **TEAM SPIRIT** series, visit our website at:

www.norwoodhousepress.com/library.aspx

On the Road

CAROLINA PANTHERS
800 South Mint Street
Charlotte, North Carolina 28202
704-358-7000
www.panthers.com

THE PRO FOOTBALL HALL OF FAME
2121 George Halas Drive NW
Canton, Ohio 44708
330-456-8207
www.profootballhof.com

On the Bookshelf

To learn more about the sport of football, look for these books at your library or bookstore:

- Frederick, Shane. *The Best of Everything Football Book.* North Mankato, Minnesota: Capstone Press, 2011.

- Jacobs, Greg. *The Everything Kids' Football Book: The All-Time Greats, Legendary Teams, Today's Superstars—And Tips on Playing Like a Pro.* Avon, Massachusetts: Adams Media Corporation, 2010.

- Editors of *Sports Illustrated for Kids. 1st and 10: Top 10 Lists of Everything in Football.* New York, New York: Sports Illustrated Books, 2011.

Index

PAGE NUMBERS IN **BOLD** REFER TO ILLUSTRATIONS.

About the Author

MARK STEWART has written more than 50 books on football and over 150 sports books for kids. He grew up in New York City during the 1960s rooting for the Giants and Jets, and was lucky enough to meet players from both teams. Mark comes from a family of writers. His grandfather was Sunday Editor of *The New York Times,* and his mother was Articles Editor of *Ladies' Home Journal* and *McCall's.* Mark has profiled hundreds of athletes over the past 25 years. He has also written several books about his native New York and New Jersey, his home today. Mark is a graduate of Duke University, with a degree in history. He lives and works in a home overlooking Sandy Hook, New Jersey. You can contact Mark through the Norwood House Press website.